CL

Body Needs

CARBOHYDRATES

for a healthy body

Heinemann Library
Chicago, Illinois

Hazel King

© 2003 Heinemann Library
a division of Reed Elsevier Inc.
Chicago, Illinois

Customer Service 888-454-2279

Visit our website at www.heinemannlibrary.com

Created by the publishing team at Heinemann Library
Designed by Ron Kamen and Celia Floyd
Illustrations by Geoff Ward
Originated by Ambassador Litho
Printed in China by Wing King Tong

07 06 05 04 03
10 9 8 7 6 5 4 3 2 1

Library of Congress Cataloging-in-Publication Data
King, Hazel.
    Carbohydrates for a healthy body / Hazel King.
        p. cm. -- (Body needs)
    Summary: Describes what carbohydrates are, what types of foods contain them, how they are digested and used to produce energy, and their role in a healthy diet.
    Includes bibliographical references and index.
ISBN 1-40340-756-8 (lib. bdg.)
ISBN 1-40343-310-0 (pbk. bdg.)
1. Carbohydrates in the body--Juvenile literature.
[1. Carbohydrates. 2. Nutrition.]   I. Title. II. Series.
  QP701.K565 2003
  612.3'96--dc21

2002012642

Acknowledgments
The author and publishers are grateful to the following for permission to reproduce copyright material: p. 4 Robert Harrison; p. 5 Tudor Photography; pp. 6, 7, 9, 13, 20, 28, 29, 38, 43 Liz Eddison; pp. 8, 11, 12, 17, 21, 23, 30, 31, 34, 35, 37, 42 Gareth Boden; p. 16 SPL/Quest; p. 24 Gettyone Stone; p. 33 Action plus; p. 36 Trevor Clifford; p. 39 Zefa; p. 40 Getty/FPG.

Cover photograph of pasta reproduced with permission of Gareth Boden.

Every effort has been made to contact copyright holders of any material reproduced in this book. Any omissions will be rectified in subsequent printings if notice is given to the publisher.

Some words are shown in bold, **like this.** You can find out what they mean by looking in the glossary.

Contents

Why Do We Need to Eat?

We all know which foods we enjoy. But have you ever stopped to wonder why we eat? Eating is not something we do just for fun. We need food to keep us alive and healthy.

Nutrients

All foods and drinks provide **energy** and **nutrients.** The main nutrients are carbohydrates, **fats,** and **proteins.** Nutrients are needed to help your body grow and repair itself. This book is about carbohydrates. You will learn what they are and how the body uses them. But you will still need to find out about the other nutrients that your body needs to be healthy. Most foods provide a mixture of different kinds of nutrients. Some provide more of one kind of nutrient than another. Your body needs nutrients every day. This is why you have to eat food. You must also drink water. Water is not a nutrient, but it is necessary for health.

Important roles

Each nutrient has an important job to do in the body. For example, carbohydrates provide the body with energy. Foods such as bread, pasta, rice, potatoes, and sugar provide you with carbohydrates. Fats also provide energy. Butter, oil, and margarine contain fats. A small amount of fat can provide a lot of energy. Foods such as meat, fish, eggs, nuts, and lentils are rich in protein. Protein is a nutrient needed to help make new **cells** throughout the body.

Eating a Variety
Of course, not all foods contain all the nutrients you need. Some have only small amounts. This is why it is important to eat a variety of foods every day.

Without the energy that food provides, leading a healthy, active life would not be possible.

The diagram here explains the different nutrients and their role in the body. Only some of the vitamins and minerals your body needs are shown.

CARBOHYDRATES provide your body with the energy you need to move and be active. They also help keep your lungs, heart, and brain working.

WATER makes up a large part of the body. It helps move substances through the body and allows **chemical reactions** to take place.

B VITAMINS help to release energy from food.

CALCIUM helps to make strong bones and teeth.

VITAMIN E helps keep the body healthy.

FATS protect your body from damage. They provide **vitamins** A, D, E, and K. They also help keep us warm and give us energy.

VITAMIN C helps to keep skin and gums healthy.

VITAMIN A helps keep the eyes and skin healthy.

VITAMIN D works with calcium to build strong bones and teeth.

PROTEIN is needed to make new cells and repair damaged ones. Protein is found in muscles, skin, and the **organs** inside your body.

IRON is important for giving blood cells their red color.

What Are Carbohydrates?

There are three types of carbohydrates found in the diet: sugar, starch, and **fiber.**

Sugars

Sugars are sometimes called "simple carbohydrates," because they are made up of very small particles, or **molecules.** A molecule is a very small part of a substance. Because they are so small, molecules of sugar are absorbed into the bloodstream very easily when we eat foods that contain sugar. Sugars can be found in food and drinks like fruits, honey, and milk. These foods contain **natural sugars.** The sugar you sprinkle on your cereal is a type of **refined sugar.** Refined sugar is added to other foods, such as cookies. All types of sugar provide your body with energy.

Starches

Starches are **complex carbohydrates.** They take longer for your body to **digest** than sugars. During digestion, all foods are broken down into molecules. When starches are broken down, they end up as molecules of **glucose.** Glucose is a sugar. So, starches are actually made up of lots of glucose molecules joined together. This means that starch also provides your body with energy. Foods containing starches include potatoes, rice, pasta, bread, and tortillas.

Carbohydrates can be found in a wide variety of foods.

Choosing Food

Today, most people can choose from a wide variety of foods. Lots of different foods are available, including frozen dinners and take-out meals.

Fiber

Fiber is the most complicated carbohydrate. Unlike sugar and starch, fiber does not provide you with energy. But it does have an important role to play during the digestion of food. Foods that provide lots of fiber include whole grain bread, brown rice, and some breakfast cereals. All fruits and vegetables, legumes (peas, beans, and lentils), oats, barley, and nuts also provide some fiber.

All the foods in this meal of pasta and vegetables, garlic bread, milk, and fruit contain carbohydrates.

Where Are the Carbohydrates in My Food?

Food	Source of Carbohydrates
cheese pizza	pizza crust and sauce
vegetable fried rice	rice and vegetables
macaroni and cheese	macaroni
hamburger	bun
lemonade or cola	sugar

Sugars and Starches

Sugars

Many people say they have a "sweet tooth," because they enjoy the taste of sweet foods. In fact, people have been sweetening foods for centuries. The ancient Romans used honey to add sweetness to food. Today, there is a huge range of different sugars available to use in food preparation.

corn syrup

fine sugar

maple syrup

powdered sugar

sugar cubes

brown sugar

honey

sugar crystals

dark sugar crystals

Sugar comes in many different forms.

The role of sugars

Sugars can be very useful when preparing foods. For example, sugars may be added to foods such as ketchup to make them more flavorful. Sugars can be used to add color to foods. For example, brown sugar will give cookies or breads a brown color. Also, when cooked, sugars will turn a golden-brown color. Sugar is used to **preserve** some foods, such as jam, and it makes food look attractive when used in frosting.

Starch Facts

When starchy foods are eaten, they are broken down into simple sugars called **glucose**. If you chew a piece of bread for a minute or so, you will find it starts to taste sweet. This is because the starch is being broken down by the saliva in your mouth.

Starches

Starches are used in very different ways from sugars in the making of food. First of all, starches are not sweet. In fact, a starch is quite bland by itself. Imagine eating a spoonful of raw flour. Most starchy foods have other ingredients added to them. For example, people add sauce to pasta, put sour cream on baked potatoes, and put butter or jam on toast.

Starches are very useful when preparing food. Starches can thicken liquids. If potatoes are added to casseroles, the sauce will become less runny. Cornstarch is another example of a starch that is used to thicken foods. It will thicken liquids, sauces, or soups.

Starches absorb, or take in, liquids. When rice or potatoes are cooked in a saucepan of water, they become soft because of the water they absorb. Starches can also help color foods. For example, bread turns a golden color when it is toasted.

These starch-rich potatoes are being cooked in a saucepan by simmering them in water. The hard, raw potatoes absorb water during cooking and become soft.

9

Complicated Fiber

Fiber is often referred to as a **complex carbohydrate**, because it has a complicated structure. The human **digestive system** is unable to break it down, so the body does not get any **nutrients** from fiber. But fiber is important because it helps the body digest food. Fiber helps make waste products soft and easy to pass out of your body.

Insoluble fiber

There are two types of fiber: **insoluble fiber** and **soluble fiber.** Insoluble fiber is found in **bran,** which is the outer layer of a grain. Foods such as whole wheat bread are made from the whole wheat grain, so the bread contains bran. Bran is known as insoluble fiber because it cannot be broken down by the human body and it does not **dissolve** in a liquid known as ethanol.

Whole grain or whole wheat products are sometimes called "unrefined" foods. These foods have been left in a fairly natural state and have not been **processed.** Wheat, for example, can be processed to make white flour by removing most of the outer bran of the wheat. White flour is used to make white bread. White flour and white bread do not contain much fiber. But if all of the wheat grain is used, including the bran and **germ,** the flour contains a lot more fiber. Insoluble fiber passes through the body without changing very much at all. It soaks up liquids inside your body, and it helps food move through your digestive system easily.

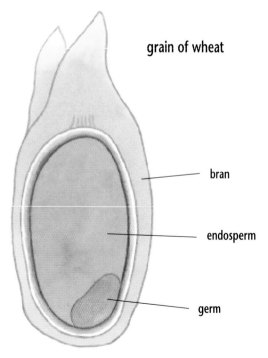

grain of wheat

bran

endosperm

germ

Fiber and Cooking

When using ingredients that contain fiber, you have to remember that they will act a bit differently. For example, if you make bread or piecrust using whole wheat flour, you must add extra liquid. The bran will soak up more liquid than white flour. Foods made with whole wheat flour will also tend to dry out more quickly than products made using white flour.

Oats are a good source of soluble fiber, so eating oatmeal for breakfast is a great start to the day.

Soluble fiber

Soluble fiber is found in foods such as oats, vegetables, and fruit. Like insoluble fiber, soluble fiber is good for your digestive system. By including plenty of fruit and vegetables in your diet, you keep your digestive system healthy. You also benefit from the various **vitamins** and **minerals** that the fruits and vegetables provide.

Some foods that include both insoluble fiber and soluble fiber include bananas, apples, oranges, pears, potatoes, kidney beans, spinach, and cooked spaghetti.

Energy Efficient

You need energy

Carbohydrates are an excellent source of **energy.** Energy is needed so your body can grow, repair itself, and keep warm. Even when you are asleep your body needs energy in order to function properly. Without energy, you would not survive. You need it to breathe, **digest** food, and think clearly. In fact, your brain is the most energy-demanding **organ** in your body.

Every **cell** in your body needs the sugar known as **glucose.** It is particularly important to your **nervous system,** red blood cells, and brain. Glucose is the sugar that carbohydrates are broken down into when they are digested. After eating foods containing carbohydrates, some of the energy will be used right away while the rest of it will be stored.

Humans use 60 calories an hour when sleeping.

Storing glycogen

Any glucose that is not needed by the body right away is stored in the **liver** or stays in the muscles. But it is not stored as glucose. Instead, it is changed into a substance known as **glycogen.** Carbohydrates are an excellent source of energy because glycogen is quickly and easily turned back into glucose as soon as it is needed.

Measuring energy

The energy that is released from food is measured in **calories.** You have probably seen calorie listings on packages of food. People can look at food labels to see how much energy will be provided by a meal or product.

Energy from food

All foods and most drinks provide energy. Water is one drink that does not supply any calories. The amount of energy supplied by a food depends on what the food contains. Foods that are high in **fat** will have a high energy value because fat provides a lot of calories.

Food type	Calories/ounce
carbohydrate	112 (4/gram)
fat	252 (9/gram)
protein	112 (4/gram)

Carbohydrates and Fats

It is interesting to compare the calories that carbohydrate foods supply by themselves and when combined with fats. For example, 3.5 ounces (100 grams) of boiled potatoes provide about 80 calories. But when potatoes are made into french fries (which means they are fried in oil), the energy values rise to 190 calories.

All foods provide energy, but different foods supply energy in different amounts. Butter is higher in energy-value than meat or bagels.

Digesting Carbohydrates

Carbohydrates are a good source of **energy.** However, until they have been broken down, your body cannot use the energy. The process of breaking down food is called digestion. After food has been **digested,** it must be absorbed in a form that can be used by your body. There are five basic stages in digestion that are explained in this chapter: chewing, swallowing, absorbing, moving, and releasing.

Chew it

The first stage of digestion takes place in your mouth. You start breaking down food with your teeth by biting and chewing the food. At the same time, chemicals called **enzymes** in your saliva start mixing with the starch. Enzymes are chemicals that speed up the breakdown of food. Large **molecules** in food are broken down into smaller ones. The saliva also makes the food moist and easier to swallow.

Swallow it

Moist, chewed-up food is then swallowed. It passes down a long tube called the **esophagus.** At the end of the esophagus is the stomach, which is sort of like a stretchy bag. Carbohydrate foods stay in the stomach for about two to three hours while being churned around and made into a mushy liquid called **chyme. Digestive juices** containing enzymes break down the food.

Absorb it

Chyme gradually passes from the stomach into the **small intestine,** where further breakdown takes place. By now, the food consists of tiny molecules, which are small enough to pass through the walls of the small intestine into the bloodstream. You will find out more about how molecules of food are absorbed on pages 16 and 17.

Move it

You can see from the diagram on page 15 that the digestive system is very long. Food cannot pass along it by itself. It needs some help. This help comes from the muscles in the walls of the intestines, which squeeze and relax, pushing the food along.

Release it

Any food that is not useful to the body will not be absorbed into the blood. Instead, it will pass from the small intestine into the **large intestine.** This is where any **insoluble fiber** will end up. As the remaining food particles travel along the large intestine, water is absorbed back into the body. Finally, waste matter is released from the body through the anus when you use the toilet.

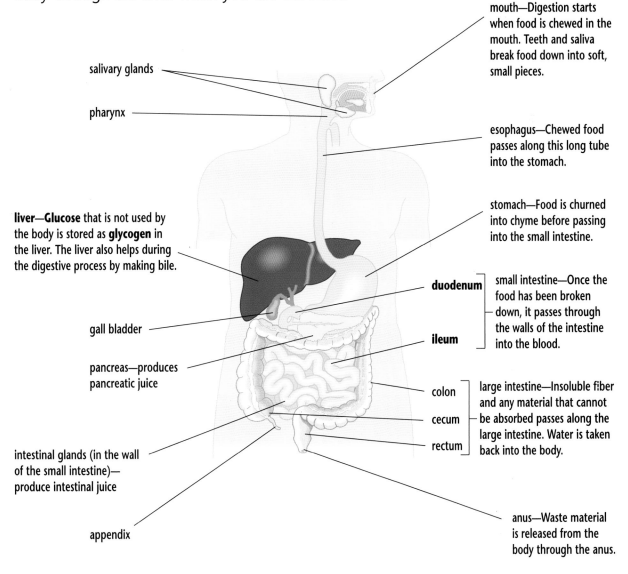

salivary glands

pharynx

liver—Glucose that is not used by the body is stored as **glycogen** in the liver. The liver also helps during the digestive process by making bile.

gall bladder

pancreas—produces pancreatic juice

intestinal glands (in the wall of the small intestine)— produce intestinal juice

appendix

mouth—Digestion starts when food is chewed in the mouth. Teeth and saliva break food down into soft, small pieces.

esophagus—Chewed food passes along this long tube into the stomach.

stomach—Food is churned into chyme before passing into the small intestine.

duodenum

ileum

small intestine—Once the food has been broken down, it passes through the walls of the intestine into the blood.

colon

cecum

rectum

large intestine—Insoluble fiber and any material that cannot be absorbed passes along the large intestine. Water is taken back into the body.

anus—Waste material is released from the body through the anus.

Food Facts
Food can take at least 24 hours to travel through the intestines. If the intestines were stretched out, they would be about as long as a school bus.

Absorbing Carbohydrates

The **nutrients** in the food that you eat need to get to all the **cells** in your body. There would be no point in eating and **digesting** food unless your body had some way of getting the food into your bloodstream and moving it around the body. The process that your body uses to do this is called absorption. This takes place in the **small intestine.**

Small intestine

By the time you are fully grown your small intestine is about 23 feet (7 meters) long. It is made up of three parts: the **duodenum**, the **jejunum**, and the **ileum.** Carbohydrates and **proteins** are absorbed in the jejunum, and **fats** are absorbed in the ileum. The small intestine looks like a folded tube that joins your stomach and your **large intestine.**

Villi

The inside lining of the small intestine is covered with tiny, fingerlike extensions called **villi.** There are millions of villi on the inside of the small intestine. The villi are about 0.02 inches (0.5 millimeters) long and have even smaller microvilli covering them. Villi increase the surface area of the small intestine.

Surface area is the space occupied by the surface of something. This is easy to measure if something is flat, like a table. But to find out the surface area of the small intestine, the folded tube would have to be straightened out and each villi would have to be flattened. This is why the surface area of the small intestine is so much bigger than it first seems.

The lining of the small intestine is covered with villi, and the villi are covered with microvilli. Here, you can see microvilli from the small intestine.

Molecules of digested food pass through the walls of the villi and into the blood vessels. It is important that food molecules are absorbed into your bloodstream so you can benefit from the nutrients. To do this, there must be as much surface area as possible to allow molecules to pass through the cell walls.

Molecules of food

When carbohydrate foods are broken down, the **glucose** molecules are absorbed through the walls of the small intestine and into the blood. The blood transports the molecules to the **liver** for processing. The food molecules include **glucose** from the breakdown of carbohydrates, **amino acids** from the breakdown of **protein**, and **fatty acids** from the breakdown of **fats**.

Leftover matter

Any food that remains after the absorption process is removed from the body. This waste contains the **fiber** that helps to keep it soft and bulky. This means it can leave the body more easily.

Your body gets water from the foods you eat and liquids you drink. Without water, the body would not be able to absorb nutrients from food.

Energy Release

Food for fuel

Your body needs fuel to provide you with **energy** in the same way a car needs gasoline to make it go. Carbohydrate foods are the best kind of "fuel" for your body because they are broken down into **glucose** that can be used by every **cell** in your body.

Your bloodstream is a bit like a car's gas tank. The bloodstream can't run on an empty tank. It needs to have a constant level of glucose for cells to use whenever energy is needed. The **liver** determines whether there is the right amount of glucose in the blood. If there is more than your body needs, the liver changes the extra glucose into **glycogen** and stores it. The liver also changes the glycogen back into glucose as soon as the glucose energy in the blood runs low.

Turning food into fuel

The process of turning food into energy is a complex one. Every cell in your body has a tiny "energy factory" where **chemical reactions** happen. The result is the release of energy. **Oxygen** is needed for the chemical reaction to take place. During this process, **carbon dioxide** and water are produced. Carbon dioxide is released in our breath when we breathe out.

The amount of energy you need depends on your weight, age, whether you are a boy or a girl, and the type and amount of activity you are doing. Children and teenagers need a lot of energy because their bodies are still growing. Boys tend to need more energy than girls, and girls tend to have more body fat than boys. Different activities need different amounts of energy. Running requires more energy than walking, but walking requires more energy than sitting.

The weather can also affect your energy levels. If the weather is cold, your body works harder trying to keep you warm.

Constant levels

The best foods for keeping your **blood sugar levels** constant are those that contain **complex carbohydrates.** These carbohydrates are slowly broken down, so they release their sugar slowly into the bloodstream. Whole grain foods, beans, fruit, and some vegetables are all slow-release carbohydrate foods. Foods such as candy and cookies, on the other hand, cause blood sugar levels to rise quickly. This makes the body try to lower the level. Blood sugar levels fall again, creating a feeling of hunger. If more sweets are eaten, the whole process starts again.

This diagram shows how energy is released from food when we eat.

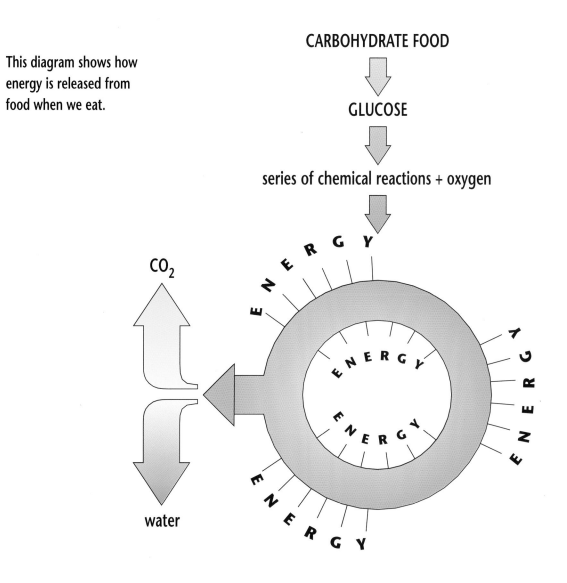

CARBOHYDRATE FOOD

GLUCOSE

series of chemical reactions + oxygen

CO_2

water

ENERGY

Energy and Exercise

The amount of **energy** you need, or **calories** you burn, just to maintain your body while you are doing absolutely nothing is known as the **basal metabolic rate (BMR).** The rate depends on the amount of muscle in the body. This means it will vary according to your height, weight, age, and whether you are a boy or a girl. The BMR for an eleven-year-old boy who is 4 feet 10 inches (1.47 meters) tall and weighs 85 pounds (38 kilograms) is 1,261 calories per day. For a girl of the same age, height, and weight, her BMR will be about 1,225 calories per day.

In and out

The energy your body gets from food is known as its energy input. The amount of energy your body uses is its output. The input and output should be about the same. However, if your energy input is higher than your output, your body will store any extra energy as **fat,** and you may gain weight. On the other hand, if your input is lower than your output, you may lose weight.

Energy Needed During Various Activities

Activity	Energy needed for one hour
running	576 calories
swimming	384 calories
walking	258 calories
sleeping	61 calories

Health experts recommend that most of your energy be provided by carbohydrate foods, such as the foods pictured.

Of course, you cannot figure out how much energy you are going to use each day and then eat the right amount of food. Usually, people listen to what their bodies tell them. They eat if they feel hungry and stop when they feel full. However, you can plan ahead if you know you are going to do a lot of exercise. For example, if you are going to be running a long race, it may be a good idea to eat meals containing carbohydrates a few days before the race.

Fuel for Sports

Kids use plenty of energy every week playing various sports like tennis, basketball, baseball, and swimming. Sports like soccer also involve a lot of running. People who play sports should know how to keep energy levels up and stay healthy. Salads and pasta are good foods to help do this. Peanut butter sandwiches are also good for this. Before playing sports, try to avoid eating foods like cake and cookies, because they are high in fat and **refined sugar.**

Body Fact

When running a **marathon**, your body starts off using blood sugar (**glucose**). Then, it uses stored-up **glycogen**. When glycogen runs out and if no other energy is supplied, the body breaks down fat or **protein** to make its energy. However, this final stage is very hard on the body.

When you eat pasta, the energy that your body receives from the food is released slowly.

Dental Health

If you often eat sugary foods, your teeth can become damaged. Sugars left in the mouth attract **bacteria** that multiply and produce **acid.** The acid can cause tooth enamel to break down and teeth to develop cavities, or holes, in them. This is known as dental caries, or tooth decay. The word *caries* means "rotten."

Brush well

After eating sugary foods, your saliva helps the mouth get rid of the acid and bacteria, but this takes about 30 minutes. For this reason, if you do eat sweets, it is better not to snack on them all day long. It is also better for your teeth if you choose sweets that can be eaten quickly. Sweets that are sucked give bacteria the conditions they need to multiply for a longer period of time, so they are more likely to cause damage. Of course, it is important to clean your teeth after eating any foods, especially sticky ones. You should brush your teeth at least twice a day.

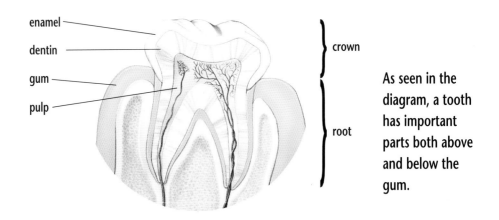

As seen in the diagram, a tooth has important parts both above and below the gum.

Inside, outside

Sugars can be divided into two groups. One group is found inside food **cells**, and the other group is not. The first group includes **glucose**, which is produced when carbohydrates are broken down, and fructose, which is found in some fruits. The second group includes honey and the **refined sugars** used in baking.

Health experts agree that a healthy diet should include only a small amount of foods containing refined sugars. This is because these sugars are found mainly in foods like cakes, cookies, pies, candy, soda pop, and many **processed** foods. These foods tend to be high in sugars (as well as **fat**) and contain few **complex carbohydrates**.

Sweet treats

It is fine to eat sweets as a treat every now and then. However, although refined sugar provides your body with energy, it does not provide any **vitamins, minerals, protein,** starches, **fiber,** or fat. Health experts recommend getting energy from foods that also provide vitamins or other **nutrients.** When you are hungry it is better to choose fruit or a sandwich instead of sweets. That way, you will also get vitamins and minerals, and it will be better for your teeth.

Always brush your teeth after eating foods containing refined sugar.

Too Much of a Good Thing

Food is the fuel you need to give you **energy,** but food can also be fun to eat. Other animals do not treat food in the same way that humans do. Animals tend to eat when they are hungry and only eat the food their body needs. People spend much more time thinking about food and shopping, cooking, and serving it. They can choose to eat at a restaurant or order meals from a take-out place. We have a great deal of choice when it comes to food.

Fast foods may be tasty, but they are often high in fat.

Carbohydrate overload

Everyone is encouraged to eat plenty of **complex carbohydrate** foods. But the trouble with many of today's meals is that they also include lots of high-**fat** foods. A burger bun, for example, is a good source of starchy carbohydrates, but the burger inside is likely to be very fatty! A sandwich on whole wheat bread sounds like a healthy idea, but if the bread is very thin and the filling includes lots of cheese and mayonnaise—both of which contain fat—then it is no longer such a healthy choice.

Healthy hearts

Many governments have worked toward improving their nation's health. One way to improve a nation's overall health is to reduce the amount of heart disease, or **coronary heart disease.** There are many reasons why people might develop heart disease. One of these is **obesity,** or being very overweight. This affects the heart and can also limit the types of activity a person can do.

The types of food available today help explain why there has been an increase in obesity and coronary heart disease. Most junk food is high in fat and sugar and contains few complex carbohydrates. Foods such as potato chips and cookies fill you up for only a short time. Soon, you feel hungry again.

Fat issue

Many people are overweight because of the large amount of fat in many of today's meals. Also, people often snack rather than eat whole meals. This makes it easier to eat too much. Many snack foods and fast foods, such as french fries and doughnuts, are fried in oil and contain a great deal of fat.

Lack of exercise

In addition to eating high-fat meals, people do not exercise as much as they used to. Instead of walking, many young people get driven to school. They spend more of their spare time doing activities that do not use much energy, such as playing video and computer games. Eating a healthy diet is important, but getting regular exercise and plenty of fresh air is also a part of staying healthy.

Staying Healthy

The **energy** supplied by starchy carbohydrate foods is very important. However, carbohydrates have many other health benefits. **Complex carbohydrates,** such as those in whole grain foods, beans, vegetables, and fruit, can help keep down the risk of problems with the **digestive system.** This is because foods containing **fiber** help waste products travel easily through the digestive system. If there are no complex carbohydrates in the diet, the waste is not able to absorb moisture and becomes hard and dry. This makes it much more difficult for the waste to leave the body, leading to problems such as constipation.

Constipation

Constipation occurs when waste matter, known as feces, becomes hard and does not travel easily through the digestive system. Sometimes this can lead to **hemorrhoids,** a condition in which the veins in the rectum become enlarged and may be painful. Another condition that can affect the digestive system is diverticulitis. Diverticulitis happens when pockets appear in the lining of the **large intestine,** or colon, and waste material gets trapped in these pockets. Eating complex carbohydrates may also help reduce the risk of getting colon cancer later in life.

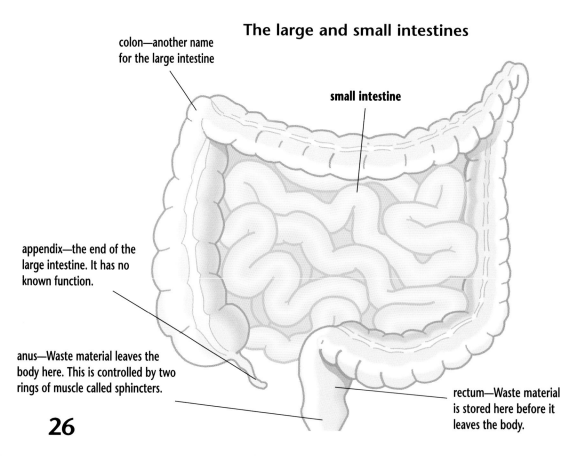

The large and small intestines

colon—another name for the large intestine

small intestine

appendix—the end of the large intestine. It has no known function.

anus—Waste material leaves the body here. This is controlled by two rings of muscle called sphincters.

rectum—Waste material is stored here before it leaves the body.

Healthy carbohydrates

Following a diet that contains plenty of healthy carbohydrates can also help reduce the chance of getting appendicitis, which is what happens when the appendix becomes infected and swollen. The appendix is a small, tubelike body part connected to the large intestine. Appendicitis is often the result of hardened waste material becoming trapped near the appendix.

Not eating enough

Not eating enough food can also be harmful. Your body needs a healthy, balanced diet so you can grow and be active and so your body can repair itself. People in **developing countries** do not always get enough food. They may suffer from diseases due to a lack of **nutrients.** Even in nations such as the United States where there should be enough food, people sometimes suffer because they are not eating the right things. People that do not have much money may buy cheap foods that do not provide a good balance and variety of nutrients. People who eat a diet low in nutrients for a long time will become ill, and their bodies will not work properly.

Labeling Sugar

Today, people are being encouraged to reduce the amount of **refined sugar** they eat, because eating too much of it can lead to health problems. This includes sugar that is added to soft drinks or used in food preparation. The **natural sugars** found in fruits and some vegetables are not linked to health problems.

All processed food products must be labeled to show their ingredients. This is useful for people who may want to avoid certain ingredients like sugar. But reading a food label is not always as easy as you might think.

It contains what?

Many of today's packaged and processed foods have extra ingredients added to them. Products such as chocolate ice cream bars, for example, have extra ingredients added to them. Sometimes **additives** called preservatives are used to make foods last longer. Other additives called stabilizers keep ingredients from separating.

Food Fact
The ingredients listed below are from a chocolate ice cream bar containing caramel and nuts. They show that both sugar and glucose syrup are present in both the caramel and the ice cream.

Ingredients: Concentrated skim milk, milk chocolate (25%), caramel (8%) (concentrated skim milk, glucose syrup, sugar, vegetable fat, butter oil, stabilizer E410), sugar, glucose syrup, vegetable fat, whey solids, wheat crispies (1%) (wheat flour, salt, raising agent E503), peanuts (1%) stabilizers, emulsifier, flavoring, color.

You may be surprised by the foods that have sugar added.

INGREDIENTS:
Tomatoes (126g per 100g Ketchup)
Spirit Vinegar, Glucose Syrup, Sugar
Salt, Spice and Herb Extracts, Spice
Garlic Powder
SUITABLE FOR A GLUTEN FREE DIET
2mg Lycopene per 10ml serving

Sugars are added to many food products. Sugar can help make foods taste better. However, you usually cannot tell exactly how much sugar is in a product just by reading the ingredients list.

Sugars are often not listed on labels as "sugar." Instead they are listed by their chemical names. For example, the following are all names of sugars: sucrose, **glucose**, lactose, fructose, maltose, corn sweetener, molasses, honey, and corn syrup. The way sugar is listed on labels is one reason people do not always know exactly what they are eating or just how much sugar is in a product.

Sweet enough?

Many foods have added sweetness without the addition of real sugar. Artificial sweeteners have been around for many years. These artificial sweeteners add sweetness without adding **calories.** Nonsugar sweeteners are particularly helpful for people with **diabetes mellitus** who must be careful about the amount of sugar they eat.

Many people use artificial sweeteners to avoid the calories in sugar, or because they have to limit the sugar in their diet.

Food Labels

The way food products are labeled is carefully controlled by law. It is important that people are not confused by a food label, especially someone who has an allergy to an ingredient.

In the United States, food products must, by law, show the following information:

- a name
- a list of ingredients, starting with the ingredient of which there is the largest amount and ending with the one of which there is the least
- the manufacturer's name and address
- a nutrition label identifying amounts of **nutrients** in the food
- serving size
- **calorie** count per serving
- instructions for use
- weight or volume of the contents

In every country around the world, food packages must be clearly labeled so people know what they are buying.

Food Fact

"Use-by" dates are used for foods that may be unsafe to eat after a certain date. These dates are found on foods such as fresh meat, fish, and cheese. "Sell-by" dates tell stores how long to display an item for sale. The product should be bought before the date expires. "Best if used by" dates are found on foods that will stay fresh longer than a few days. They will not be at their best after this date. These dates are found on breakfast cereals, cookies, and canned foods.

What's in a name?

All packaged food must have a name that tells people exactly what is in the package. For example, the label could not just say "bread" because there are lots of different types of bread. Instead, the label might say "rye bread," "100% whole wheat bread," or "sourdough bread."

Reading labels

You can also find different starches listed in ingredients lists. For example, starches such as flour can thicken sauces. Thickeners, or **thickening agents,** are often used in reduced-sugar or low-sugar products. Sugar usually makes things thicken, so when less sugar is used, something else is needed to act as a thickening agent. Cornstarch and potato starch are thickeners that you often see listed on food labels.

Starch is needed to thicken food products, such as this sauce being used to make a casserole. Starches are often listed on food labels.

Sugar Control

Glucose is your body's main source of energy. The way your body uses glucose is controlled by several chemicals called hormones. One of these hormones is known as insulin. Diabetics, or people who have the disease diabetes mellitus, are not able to use glucose normally. Their bodies are either not able to make enough insulin or their bodies are not able to respond to it the way they should. This means their bodies cannot control their blood sugar level. The amount of glucose traveling around in their blood can become very high or very low.

Diabetes mellitus

A very high or very low level of glucose in the blood is serious. Diabetes mellitus can be controlled by either making changes to the diet or by taking medicine and insulin. Some diabetics need a daily injection of insulin, while others get along fine as long as they are very careful about what they eat. A diet high in complex carbohydrates and fiber is recommended because these foods help control the rate at which sugar is absorbed into the blood. Such foods as whole grain bread, brown rice, vegetables, and fruit would be part of a diet high in fiber and complex carbohydrates.

Sweet treats

Someone with diabetes must make sure they do not eat too much sugar or sugary foods and drinks. Sugary products will cause a sudden rise in blood sugar levels. However, they do not have to avoid sweet foods completely. They can eat sweet treats occasionally, but it is better for them to eat them after a meal rather than on an empty stomach. They can also eat products such as "diabetic chocolate" made especially for people with diabetes. These products do not have sugar in them, but they often contain just as much fat and calories as the regular versions.

Young and old

It is not clear why people develop diabetes. There are two types of diabetes: insulin-dependent diabetes, which is also known as juvenile-onset diabetes, and non-insulin-dependent diabetes, which is also known as adult-onset diabetes. Insulin-dependent diabetes usually strikes people who are younger than 40. Symptoms may develop suddenly and include being very thirsty and needing to urinate much more often than normal. People with this type of diabetes need to take insulin every day.

People with non-insulin-dependent diabetes do not need treatment with insulin. Their bodies still produce insulin. This type of diabetes can be controlled by eating healthy foods or sometimes with medicine. This type tends to develop in people age 40 and over, but anyone who is overweight is more at risk of developing the disease as they get older.

Living with Diabetes

Young people who have diabetes often learn they have the disease because of things that happen at school. They might have trouble concentrating and feel very thirsty all the time, They might have to use the bathroom frequently. At mealtimes, they also might not feel very hungry.

Of course, having diabetes does not have to ruin people's lives. Diabetics are still able to enjoy sports like soccer, hockey, or skiing. The main change diabetics have to make to their diets is avoiding snacks and desserts. It is also recommended that they eat lots of complex carbohydrates, such as rice and pasta.

Having diabetes can make you change the types of food you eat, but you can still enjoy a wide variety of sports.

Food Allergies

A food allergy is a reaction caused by eating a certain food or foods. Examples of foods and drinks likely to cause an allergic reaction include milk, eggs, fish, shellfish, nuts, and soybeans. Gluten is a substance found in wheat, which is used to make flour, a carbohydrate food. Celiac disease is the name for an intolerance to gluten.

Gluten

Gluten is a **protein** found mainly in wheat, although it is also in rye, barley, oats, and corn. People with celiac disease have a condition in which the walls of their **small intestine** become damaged if they eat gluten. When the **villi** in the lining of the small intestine are damaged, **nutrients** are not absorbed properly. The symptoms include stomach pain, tiredness, bloating, diarrhea, and weight loss.

Avoiding foods

Someone with celiac disease must avoid all foods containing gluten. Unfortunately, this includes a huge range of foods because wheat is in so many things. Just think how many products are made from wheat flour: cookies, cakes, most breads, pancakes, pasta, and pastries.

Anyone with celiac disease should not eat these foods. They all contain gluten.

Lots of **processed** foods such as desserts, snacks, and frozen dinners have starch-based thickeners containing gluten. These must be avoided, too. Also, anything containing rye, barley, or corn may cause a reaction, as well as foods made using oats, such as oatmeal and many cold breakfast cereals.

Gluten-free products

Fortunately, many supermarkets and health-food stores sell a variety of gluten-free products, including breads, cakes, and pasta. These foods have gluten-free labels to show that they are safe for people with celiac disease to eat.

Food Fact
People with celiac disease need to avoid some or all of the following: barley, bran, malt, modified food starch, oats, rye, pasta, and wheat flour. This means they must read food labels very carefully.

Some foods are labeled "gluten free."

Staple Starches

A staple food is the main food of a diet. It is usually a food that provides **energy.** In many countries, starchy carbohydrate foods are staple foods because they form a major part of a country's diet. Different countries and cultures have their own staples depending on their climate and what they are able to grow. One of the staple foods in the United States is wheat. Back in the 1800s, pioneers who settled in the Great Plains states such as Kansas and Nebraska found that wheat grew very well there. Today, the United States is one of the world's leading wheat producers, and the Great Plains are sometimes referred to as the "nation's breadbasket."

Today we have a huge variety of breads to choose from.

Potatoes for all

Potatoes are also one of the staple foods Americans eat. Idaho and Washington are major potato-growing states. Potatoes are full of **nutrients** and can be fixed many different ways. Popular potato dishes include mashed potatoes, french fries, potato pancakes, and hash browns. Many people in the U.S. would not consider a meal complete unless it was served with potatoes.

Many choices

We do not have to rely only on foods that can be grown and produced in one country. There are many ways to **preserve** food so that it will keep longer, even when the food is shipped from another country. This means you have a much wider choice of foods available. You can buy mangoes grown in Brazil, rice noodles from Thailand, olives from Greece, or basmati rice from India. Some of these foods are also now grown or manufactured in the United States.

Pass the pasta

Pasta is a staple food of Italy. It is also very popular in the United States. Pasta is made with flour. Sometimes eggs are added. The flour used for pasta making comes from durum wheat. Durum wheat is ground up to make semolina flour, which is gritty and yellow. Once the pasta dough has been made, it is cut, pressed, and molded into different shapes and sizes.

Pasta parties

Pasta is a healthy food. It is low in **fat** and high in **complex carbohydrates.** If you buy pasta made from whole wheat, the pasta is also a good source of **fiber.** Many athletes eat pasta before a big event—they may even have a pasta party the evening before.

Pasta comes in a variety of shapes, sizes, and colors.

Worldwide Diets

Rice is a staple food in many countries, including India, China, and Japan. Like pasta, rice is low in **fat** and high in **complex carbohydrates**. Brown rice still has its outer layer of **bran**. So it also provides **fiber** and has slightly more **protein**, iron, calcium, and B **vitamins**.

Food Facts

Long grain rice is about four to five times longer than it is wide. This is the kind of rice used in most rice dishes.

Short grain rice has short, plump grains. It tends to stay moist and the grains cling together when cooked. Short grain rice is the kind of rice used in rice pudding.

Rice dishes

There are many different varieties of rice. So it is not surprising that there are also many different ways of cooking and serving rice. In the United States, for example, rice is used in many dishes such as jambalaya and chicken and rice. In India, long grain rice is cooked with meat, fish, or vegetables to make a dish called biryani. Japanese and Chinese dishes tend to use soft, sticky rice that can be shaped with the fingers or picked up with chopsticks. The Italians are famous for risotto. Small amounts of broth are slowly added to the risotto rice until it becomes creamy, plump, and tender.

Polenta is made from corn and can be used to make corn bread.

Gluten free

Like pasta, rice is a "slow-release" carbohydrate, so it is a much better source of **energy** than the "instant" energy provided by sugary foods. In addition, people with celiac disease can eat rice, because it does not contain any gluten.

Puffed rice

Rice is often eaten in its natural grain form. But it can also be **processed** to make many other products. Grains of rice can be ground up to turn them into rice flour, ground rice, and flaked rice. These ingredients are then used to make puddings, cakes, cookies, and **thickening agents** for soups or stews. Rice can also be "puffed" to make rice cereals and rice cake snacks.

Moroccan couscous

Couscous is another kind of rice. It cooks very quickly in hot water or by being steamed. You can buy packages of dried couscous, some of which have flavors already added to them. Traditionally, couscous was a staple food of north African countries such as Morocco.

Corn

Corn is a staple food of many countries including Italy and Mexico. You can eat it straight off the cob. Or it can be used to make a wide variety of products, such as tortillas, corn bread, corn chips, and breakfast cereals. Polenta, a dough made from cornmeal, can also be made from corn.

People often use couscous instead of rice.

Eating for Health

Most people would like to be healthy and free from disease all the time. This is important, not just for individuals but for all of society. It is better for everyone to prevent diseases from happening rather than treating them once people are ill.

Food Fact

Experts agree that the key to a healthy diet is to eat a variety of foods. For most people this means eating:

- lots of fruits and vegetables. You can choose from fresh, frozen, canned, dried, or juices.
- more bread, grains, and potatoes. These should make up at least one-third of your diet.
- less fat and sugar.

Preventing disease

The foods you eat during your lifetime can affect your chances of getting serious diseases such as **coronary heart disease. Dietary guidelines** have been set to help people choose a diet made of foods needed for good health. These guidelines suggest different ways to follow a healthy diet. Dietary guidelines are made by various health organizations and governments.

Varied diet

Eating a variety of different foods is especially important. People sometimes end up eating the same foods every day out of habit, laziness, or just because they like them. But in the long run, this can lead to a lack of some **nutrients** and could cause health problems. There is not one single food that contains all the nutrients in the right amounts, which is why everyone should eat a variety of foods. When you think about the thousands of foods available, you should not really have a problem finding different ones that you like to eat.

Drinking plenty of water is part of a healthy diet.

The Food Guide Pyramid

To help Americans understand healthful eating, the U.S. government developed the Food Guide Pyramid. It is used by **dieticians,** health professionals, manufacturers, and schools. The Food Guide Pyramid clearly shows the kinds of foods that should be included in a healthy diet and in what amounts. For example, the largest part of the pyramid is the bread, cereal, rice, and pasta group—all carbohydrate foods. The smallest part of the pyramid is fats, oils, and sweets, which it recommends that people eat "sparingly," or in small quantities.

The Food Guide Pyramid shown below was created to give you an idea of what to eat each day to maintain a healthful diet.

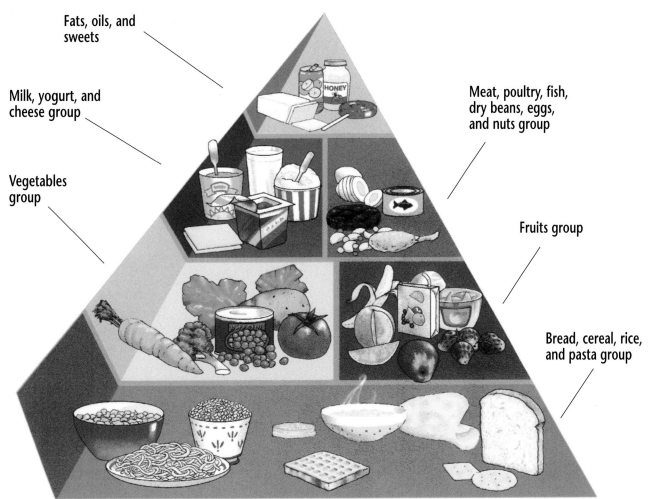

Fats, oils, and sweets

Milk, yogurt, and cheese group

Vegetables group

Meat, poultry, fish, dry beans, eggs, and nuts group

Fruits group

Bread, cereal, rice, and pasta group

Achieving a Balance

Eating a healthy diet is not limited to the foods you choose. It is also about the way those foods are prepared and cooked. Potatoes are high in **complex carbohydrates** and provide **vitamin** C. But if potatoes are cut up and deep-fried, they will also contain lots of **fat.** Or, if the potatoes are boiled then left to go cold and reheated, the vitamin C is likely to be lost. This is because vitamin C **dissolves** into the cooking water and is destroyed by heat. So, it is important to think about how foods are cooked.

Good-bye to french fries?

Eating a healthy, balanced diet does not mean you have to give up all fatty foods. It just means you should not eat them all the time. For example, eating french fries is fine once in a while. But they are high in fat. If you get fries with a burger, you might try splitting the order of fries with a friend. That way you will both end up eating less fat.

Foods cooked without using or adding fat can be delicious. Eggs are a good example. They can be boiled, poached, or scrambled. Different meats can be cooked on a grill. If you're just looking for a snack, a ripe banana, raisins, or mixed fruit taste sweet. They will also give you more energy in the long run and less fat than **refined sugars.**

Potatoes can be eaten in a variety of ways.

Saving vitamins

You can get more benefits from food prepared in the proper manner. For example, when vegetables are cooked by boiling them in water, some vitamins dissolve into the water and are lost when the vegetables are drained. It is better to steam or microwave vegetables. Less water is needed, and more of the vitamins are saved.

A healthy, balanced diet should be part of everyone's lifestyle.

Carbohydrates in a variety of foods, broken down into starch, sugars, and fiber.

Food (ounces = oz grams = g)	Starch	Sugar	Fiber
1 banana	0.5 oz (15.3 g)	0.05 oz (1.5 g)	0.07 oz (2.0 g)
3.5 ounces (100 grams) cauliflower	0.007 oz (0.2 g)	0.06 oz (1.8 g)	0.06 oz (1.6 g)
2 slices whole grain bread	1.45 oz (41.3 g)	0.11 oz (3 g)	0.21 oz (5.9 g)
2 slices white bread	1.54 oz (43.8 g)	0.11 oz (3 g)	0.13 oz (3.7 g)
3.5 ounces (100 grams) white flour	2.69 oz (76.2 g)	0.05 oz (1.5 g)	0.13 oz (3.6 g)

Information adapted from Bender, David A. *Food Tables & Labelling.* Oxford University Press, 1999.

Glossary

acid chemical compound that aids in digestion

additive substance (natural or artificial) added to foods to increase their shelf life or to improve their color, flavor, or texture

amino acid smaller unit or building block of proteins. Different amino acids combine together to form a protein.

bacteria microscopic living things. Some are helpful, like those in our intestines, but some can cause disease.

basal metabolic rate (BMR) rate at which the body uses food when it is at rest to obtain energy, build tissue, and dispose of waste material

blood sugar level amount of glucose in the blood. This will rise after sugar has been eaten and will slowly fall until food is eaten again.

bran the outer layer of a grain

calorie measurement of energy supplied by food

carbon dioxide one of the gases in the air. Animals breathe out carbon dioxide.

cell smallest unit of a plant or animal

chemical reaction when two or more chemicals react together to produce a change

chyme mushy liquid that passes from the stomach to the small intestine

complex carbohydrate type of carbohydrate that is made of many simple carbohydrates linked together. Starches such as potatoes contain complex carbohydrates.

coronary heart disease condition in which the blood vessels leading to the heart become blocked by fatty substances and the blood cannot get to the heart as easily

developing country poorer country that does not have well-established industries or services

diabetes mellitus disease in which the body cannot control the level of sugar in the blood

dietary guideline suggestion for healthy eating

dietician person who advises people about what they eat

digest to break down and change food into simpler forms that the body can use

digestive juice liquid containing enzymes that helps break down food during digestion

digestive system all the parts of the body that are used to digest food

dissolve break down or mix with a liquid so that the liquid is the same throughout

duodenum   first part of the small intestine

energy   ability to do work or to make something happen

enzyme   substance that helps a chemical reaction take place faster

esophagus   tube through which food travels from the mouth to the stomach

fat   substance found in a wide range of foods. The body can change fat into energy. Fat is stored by the body in a layer below the skin.

fatty acid   kind of acid found in animal fat and vegetable oils and fats

fiber   substance found in plants that cannot be digested by the human body

germ   (of wheat or corn) central part of grain that contains oil

glucose   simple form of sugar that is broken down from carbohydrate food during digestion

glycogen   substance made from glucose that is stored in the liver and muscles following absorption

hemorrhoids   swollen veins around the rectum, often caused by a diet low in fiber

hormone   substance made by different glands in the body that affects or controls certain organs, cells, or tissues

ileum   third and last part of the small intestine

insoluble fiber   type of fiber that cannot be broken down by the human digestive system, such as the bran in whole wheat bread

jejunum   middle part of the small intestine

large intestine   part of the intestines through which undigested food passes after it has left the small intestine

liver   organ in the body that plays a role in digestion. It makes bile and helps clean the blood. People also eat beef and chicken livers, which are a rich source of vitamins and minerals.

marathon   26-mile (42-kilometer) race

mineral   nutrient found in foods that the body needs to stay healthy

molecule   smallest unit of a substance that is still that same substance and still has the same properties as the substance

natural sugar   type of sugar naturally present in foods such as fruit

nervous system   series of connected nerves throughout the body

nutrient   substance found in foods that helps the body grow and stay healthy. Carbohydrates, proteins, fats, vitamins, and minerals are all nutrients.

obesity   state of being extremely overweight

organ   body part that has a particular job to do. An eye is an example of an organ.

oxygen   gas present in the air and used by the body. Oxygen is one of the most common elements and is used by the body to make amino acids.

preserve   to protect food from spoiling

processed   describes foods that have been changed to make them easier to prepare or cook

protein   complex chemical that the body needs to grow and repair cells

refined sugar   type of sugar added to foods to make them sweet. Refined sugar comes from the processing of sugar beets or sugarcane. It provides energy, but all the vitamins and minerals have been removed.

small intestine   part of the intestine into which food passes from the stomach to be digested and absorbed into the blood. Undigested food passes right through the small intestine into the large intestine.

soluble fiber   fiber that dissolves in water and passes into the blood

thickening agent   something that helps a food product set and gives it shape and structure

urinate   pass liquid waste out of the body

villus   tiny, fingerlike extensions in the small intestine through which digested food and water are absorbed. More than one villus are called villi.

vitamin   nutrient needed by the body in small amounts

Further Reading

Ballard, Carol. *The Digestive System.* Chicago: Heinemann Library, 2002.

Brownlie, Ali. *Why Are People Vegetarian?* Austin, Tex.: Raintree Publishers, 2002.

D'Amico, Joan, and Karen Eich Drummond. *The Healthy Body Cookbook.* Hoboken, N.J.: John Wiley & Sons, 1999.

Gregson, Susan R. *Healthy Eating.* Mankato, Minn.: Capstone Press, 2000.

Hardie, Jackie. *Blood and Circulation.* Chicago: Heinemann Library, 1998.

Kalbacken, Joan. *The Food Pyramid.* Danbury, Conn.: Children's Press, 1998.

Landau, Elaine. *Wheat.* Danbury, Conn.: Children's Press, 1999.

Landau, Elaine. *Sugar.* Danbury, Conn.: Children's Press, 1999.

Royston, Angela. *Eating and Digestion.* Chicago: Heinemann Library, 1998.

Westcott, Patsy. *Diet and Nutrition.* Austin, Tex.: Raintree Publishers, 2000.

Index